The Baristas Ultimate Guide to Coffee

by Alonso Ibarra
BoldBarista.com

The Baristas Ultimate Guide to Coffee

COPYRIGHT

COPYRIGHT NOTICE

© Copyright 2015 by BOLDBARISTA. All Rights Reserved. This guide may not be reproduced or transmitted in any form without the written permission of the author. Every effort has been made to make this guide as complete and accurate as possible. Although the author has prepared this guide with the greatest of care, and have made every effort to ensure the accuracy, we assume no responsibility or liability for errors, inaccuracies or omissions. Before you begin, check with the appropriate authorities to insure compliance with all laws and regulations. This book is meant for educational purposes only.

The purpose of this ebook is to educate. The author does not warrant that the information contained herein is fully complete and shall not be responsible for any errors or omissions. The author shall have neither liability nor responsibility to any person or entity with respect to any loss or damage caused or alleged to be caused directly or indirectly by this guide, nor do we make any claims or promises of your ability become a barista by using this information.

Visit www.boldbarista.com

FOREWORD

You love coffee. Yet, there are times as you stroll down the aisles at supermarkets, or at coffee shops, you get confused by the lingo and jargon used in the coffee world. It strikes you that you ought to learn more about your favorite drink, for you feel the need to be a complete part of this world. You want to master the vocabulary to speak the coffee language, to learn more about coffee because you know coffee is more than just a drink. If you feel this way, and I guess you do because that's why you have this book in your hands, then right here in your hands is a comprehensive guide to the world's favorite drink. Here is a book that will answer all those coffee questions that have been nagging you at the back of your mind.

The Barista's Ultimate Guide is written in a simple and enjoyable way, to help you find out about the history of coffee and how it has gone from a regional specialty to a worldwide commodity. You will learn how drinks prepared from coffee evolved and how technology has changed the way we consume them.

We will look at how to identify where your beans come from just by the taste. We will look at the way coffee is roasted and learn why we roast coffee to different specifications. Grinding coffee at home is a valid shortcut to achieve outstanding coffee and as we go through these pages together, will see why.

Whoever you are, wherever you are from, I want you to start feeling empowered to make healthy choices with your coffee, knowing what is good and separating out the bad to stop being fleeced by marketeers. After reading this, you will step into any coffee shop not only knowing your onions but also knowing that things are going just the right way.

Then we move on to the different ways of brewing coffee at home. We will learn about different equipment, some you already know, and others that could be new to you. You will learn to make cold-brew as well!

I can guarantee you that after reading this book, you will be able to make the kind of coffee you find in the best cafes around the world; the kind of coffee that retails for a price that makes you want to cry, but trust me, you will be laughing as you make barista-quality coffee at home. I know that you will be able to impress your friends and family after we are through with the journey through these pages filled with so much coffee knowledge. You will be an expert in no time at all!

Plus, you will find the best tips and techniques used by baristas that you can apply in your very own kitchen!

Visit our blog at www.boldbarista.com to find a collection of 22 tried and tested recipes to try at home, stay up to date, and learn more about coffee.

The Baristas Ultimate Guide to Coffee

Contents

HISTORY OF COFFEE

5

THE BEAN

15

THE ROAST

35

THE GRIND

44

TASTING

54

MILK WATER SUGAR

60

BREW THE PERFECT COFFEE

66

SUSTAINABILITY

77

The Baristas Ultimate Guide to Coffee

PART ONE

HISTORY OF COFFEE

COFFEE STORY

"Just the other day, I was in my neighborhood Starbucks, waiting for the post office to open. I was enjoying chocolatey cafe mocha when it occurred to me that to drink a mocha is to gulp down the entire history of the New World. From the Spanish exportation of Aztec cacao, and the Dutch invention of the chemical process for making cocoa, on down to the capitalist empire of Hershey, PA, and the lifestyle marketing of Seattle's Starbucks, the modern mocha is a bittersweet concoction of imperialism, genocide, invention, and consumerism served with whipped cream on top."
— Sarah Vowell (author, journalist, essayist and social commentator)

Just hearing the word 'coffee' reminds me of a lovely mornings watching the world go by with a cup in my hands. The word is said to originate from the Arabic qahhwat. It must have had to travel quite a bit to become the word we know today. In Turkey its kahve, via the Dutch word koffie (the Dutch were first to import it into Europe).

Today, it is an international word for a drink, a place, or a meeting. Either way, my day doesn't start until I have had my first cup! In this chapter, we will discuss coffee drinking through the ages, how it has come to be an international commodity unlike any other. We will also discuss the challenges faced by coffee growers in recent times and what we can do to make our coffee habits more sustainable.

You can also find out more information by visiting the blog at www.boldbarista.com

FROM ETHIOPIA TO THE WORLD

There are several legends about how coffee was discovered and its first uses. You might read about it being attributed to the Yemeni Sufi mystic, Abu al-Hasan al-Shadhili. The story says that he watched as birds eating red berries became revitalized, which led him to investigate and discover the beans' properties.

The most popular legend is about the Ethiopian goat herder, Kaldi, who is said to have eaten the red coffee berries after he noticed his herd of goats prancing around energetically after consuming the same fruit. The same legend tells how Kaldi brought the berries to a monastery where monks cleaned and roasted the beans. They supposedly created an elixir by steeping the toasted beans in water.

These myths are probably far from what happened. It seems far more likely that the cherry would have been a source of food at that time. Through experimentation, people came to the realization that the beans contained beneficial nutrients and probably steeped the green beans in water to create the coffee elixir that would have been drunk at that time. Coffee roasting was not introduced until the 16th century when Turkish coffee is said to have been created. Coffee houses existed in Constantinople around 1550, and it is believed they faced religious opposition as was the case also when they extended into Christian capitals.

In all of this myth and stories, one thing is sure - this coffee elixir was widely used throughout the Arabian territory, and was regarded as a brain tonic or "blessed wine." It stayed within the region, not reaching Europe until the 16th century.

You have heard of Arabica coffee (or Coffea Arabica in Latin). The Latin name was so given to this coffee plant precisely because it was widely cultivated throughout that region. Most of the coffee we consume today comes from Arabica coffee bushes, although nowadays they are grown in other parts of the world.

Coffea Canephora, or Robusta, is the other widely cultivated coffee bush. It was only discovered in Belgian Congo in 1890, growing in the wild. The Belgian horticultural firm named it Coffea Robusta and cultivated it into some different varieties, one of which became very successful and is now widely cultivated. It is the second most popular species regarding production. We'll discuss the differences between these and other varieties in more details as we go on.

COFFEE COMES TO EUROPE

Mokha, a city in Yemen, enjoyed the coffee trade of the world for two hundred years. It was the arrival of Dutch traders to the Arabian territory in the 16th century (which was later the Dutch East India Company) that led to the mass consumption we know today.

The Dutch traders saw the opportunities to profit from bringing this "new" product to European customers, but it was not going to be easy. It's documented that the Arab rulers were not keen on sharing the secrets of cultivating coffee. Coffee was a gift from the gods. They referred to it as blessed wine, and they did not want it leaving the region. That was not going to stop the Dutchmen, who decided to smuggle some unroasted coffee beans back to Amsterdam. These beans they brought back from Mocha produced healthy plants in the Dutch greenhouses.

How come coffee is grown in Indonesia? Well, Holland did not have the right climate for producing coffee, so the powerful East India Company brought coffee to Indonesia, to the island of Java. These coffee plantations are still in operation, and "Java" is synonymous with coffee for many people.

And what about the Americas? The Dutch gifted a live coffee tree to the French king, Louis XIV, who took it west to the Caribbean, to the island Reunion in 1715, Central America, and Mexico. The excellent conditions for growing coffee in the Dutch and French colonies allowed coffee to become a commodity, a widely traded good amongst all irrespective of class or status as opposed to the beginning when it was a luxury or a reserve of nobility.

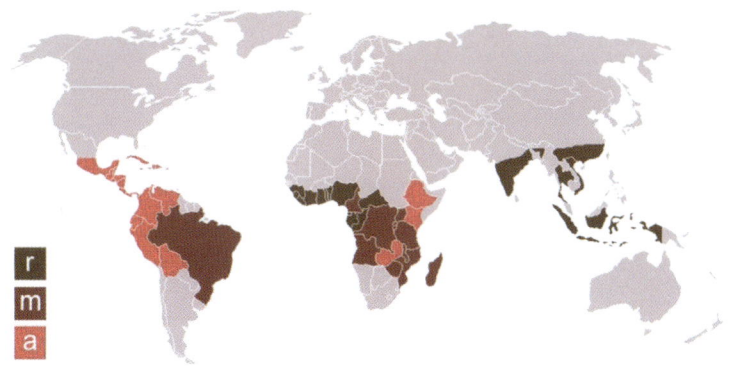

Map showing areas of production. Some countries only grow Robusta varietals ('r') and others specialize in Arabica ('a'). Other countries can grow both

FIRST COFFEE SHOPS

The first coffee shop in Europe is believed to have been one started by a military officer in Vienna, where the custom of adding milk and sugar started. (You will find a recipe for a 'Melange' or Viennese coffee later on in this book.)

Did you know: When coffee was first introduced into Venice it became popular quickly, but some people argued that it should be banned because they claimed it was a 'pagan' product, imported from pagan lands. They may have been scared at the effect coffee had on its drinkers. They urged the Catholic Church to do something about it. They wanted it banned from import. Luckily for all, the pope at the time was already an aficionado who liked his cup of coffee. He said it would be a sin to outlaw such a delicious drink!

A 17th-century coffee house in London

London's first coffee shop opened in 1652, and by 1663 there were 82. It took a hundred years for coffee shops to get from the Constantinople to the Thames, but when it arrived it did with an explosion! A whole new industry had been created where people could drink, meet, discuss, joke, do business, gossip, and be creative.

Each of these early coffee shops was unique. For example, in Clerkenwell Green, you could drink coffee and have a haircut. In Covent Garden, you could drink and browse a catalog of escorts. In Chelsea, the interior was filled with fine examples of taxidermy. Coffee shop on a boat? There was one moored in front of Somerset House, and you could watch dancers and jugglers perform while you sipped your coffee. Twenty-five years later, Charles II, issued a royal edict against public coffee houses because they were 'places where the disaffected met and spread scandalous reports about the Monarchy.' He was forced to withdraw it!

The coffee house was imported to the USA with the same format as those in England. The Green Dragon Tavern in Boston (also a Freemason Lodge) served coffee and was also the birthplace of the American

Revolution. One coffee house, The Tontine Coffee House in New York, was an important meeting place for the city's business community. The site later housed the New York Stock Exchange.

As many Italian immigrants moved into the young new country, they brought their coffee culture with them. These Italian coffee houses sold Espresso and pastries just like they did in continental Europe. Coffee houses in the US took on a new role in the community as an entertainment venue, allowing aspiring singers and poets to perform, serving up Espresso and food, allowing the youth a place to meet and socialize and have fun. Thus, the modern coffee shop concept was born.

POPULARITY SURGES

Chicory root is a coffee additive in colonial America, still popular today in parts of the USA. Instant coffee pre-mixed with milk and sugar helped make coffee the preferred hot drink in the US. Both pictures above are adverts from 1880's

In the early 1900's, the per capita consumption in the US was under 5 kilos per year. In the Netherlands, it was more than 7 kilos. Instant coffee was widely available for home preparation. At the time, Brazil produced about three-fourths of the world's coffee crop. Followed in order of importance by Venezuela, Colombia, Guatemala, Mexico, Haiti, Salvador, and Indonesia. Just like today, most of the coffee was being prepared in the home.

COFFEE INDUSTRY TODAY

Today, the biggest consumers of coffee in the world are in Europe. Consumer data research carried out by Euromonitor estimates that Finland consumes almost 10 kilos of coffee per capita per year. That is a quite a lot of Espressos! Research shows that the Dutch drink about 2.4 cups per day or almost 7 kilos per person per year. Takeaway coffee in Nordic countries like Denmark and Norway are the most expensive in the world too. It is not just workers who are consuming coffee outside the home. There's also friends meeting to catch up, and busy shoppers taking a break, people sitting down to use free Wi-Fi. The cafe of today is for everyone!

The world's largest coffee producing nation is Brazil, but most of the coffee produced there is Robusta. Robusta is the most imported variety of coffee into the UK. The UK coffee shop industry wasworth over £5.8 billion in 2013, and with annual growth that exceeds most other industries. Worldwide coffee trade alone is worth $20 billion, and the whole industry is estimated to be worth $100 billion!

Hard to believe that most coffee producers still live at or close to the poverty line.

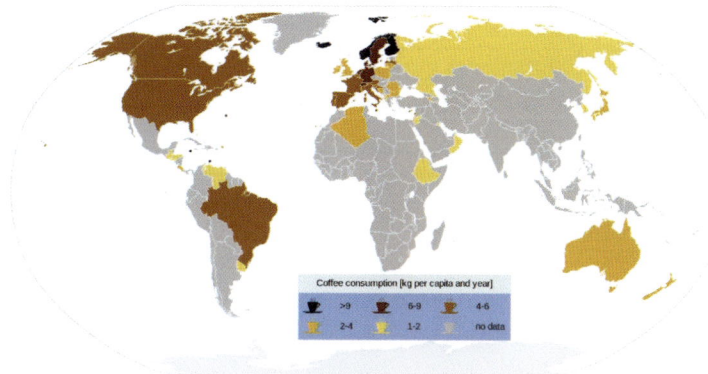

Map showing coffee consumption per capita per annum (for those countries where data is collected)

COFFEE FACTS

Many studies have been conducted to assess the effects of coffee on humans. These help us understand its beneficial properties and the reason why it is still one of, if not the most, craved drink around the world.

Coffee is not considered a health food nor is it a necessary dietary component. However, it has been proven to contain antioxidants, even after roasting.

Coffee affects the nervous system, heightens memory capacity as well as the ability to learn by increasing concentration. It reduces tiredness and increases sensory perception. It affects the brain by increasing the reaction times (you could say it makes you quicker). It increases heart rate and circulation, making your breathing more efficient.

Your muscles are affected by coffee too. It can improve your coordination and help you feel less tired during workouts. Coffee helps your stomach digest food by stimulating certain nerves in your gut. It helps your liver produce more bile (the stuff in your gut that contributes to digest fat) and stimulates your metabolism glands. And as we have probably all experienced, it increases diuresis (it makes you wee).

PART TWO

THE BEAN

ESSENTIAL BEAN FACTS

Almost all my middle-aged and elderly acquaintances, including me, feel about 25 unless we haven't had our coffee, in which case we feel 107. - Martha Beck (author and sociologist)

I just love making coffee at home; there is something like a little ritual I go through every time I prepare coffee. From getting my equipment ready, putting all the ingredients together, getting the cups right plus any sugar and milk. I say 'just one more cup' before I can get on with whatever is going on that day.

In this chapter, you will learn more about where coffee comes from and how you can differentiate coffee origins visually and by taste and smell. Let us begin with the coffee plant.

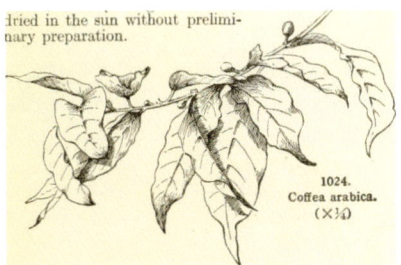

The coffee plant is a hardy perennial bush which produces bright red berries. The fruit is a small fleshy berry and contains two seeds enclosed in a thin parchment-like shell, each seed being rounded on the outside and flat with a furrow on the inside. Although they are not actual beans, they are so called because their look is similar to that of a common bean

All coffee plants are evergreen shrubs that grow up to five meters tall when allowed to grow freely, but in a cultivated state, it is seldom permitted to grow higher than 3 meters to facilitate the gathering of the berries. Its leaves are smooth, dark green and glossy on the surface but paler beneath.

The flowers are small and appear in clusters of white at the bases of the leaves. They are very fragrant and give the shrub a beautiful appearance. When the flowers die, they are succeeded by numerous little red fleshy berries that resemble small cherries, each of which contains two of the seeds commonly called coffee.

It can take Arabica berries from six to eight months to ripen, and Robusta can take from nine to eleven months. Usual methods of making new plants include cuttings, grafting, and germination. With the right conditions, coffee plants are very easy to grow. Originally cultivated in Yemen, coffee shrubs are now cultivated around the globe (between the Tropic of Capricorn and the Tropic of Cancer).

Within these areas that coffee can grow, other aspects are preferential to each variety:

- Sub-Tropical regions: Excellent yearly growth rate of the Arabica species is favored at medium altitude with defined rainy and dry seasons.
- Equatorial regions: Higher altitude with continuous rainfall, allow for continuous production, thus having more than one harvest per year. Higher altitude Arabica beans are highly acclaimed.
- Lower altitude: These regions are hotter and more humid. They are not suitable for Arabica shrubs but are the ideal conditions for Robusta plants.

The structure of coffee berry and beans:
1. Centre.
2. Bean.
3. Silver skin.
4. Parchment.
5. Pectin layer.
6. Pulp.
7. Outer skin.

The coffee fruit is divided into two main parts, the pericarp, and the seed. Coffee seed or the 'bean' is about 10mm long and 6mm wide.

Pericarp

The pericarp is the outer part of the fruit (everything but the bean); the skin, mucilage and the parchment. The skin or exocarp is the outer layer of green which then changes as the fruit matures.

Color depends on the coffee variety and is most commonly red or yellow. The mucilage or pulp is the flesh of the coffee fruit. In the wet processing method, the mucilage is removed through controlled fermentation steeped in water. In the dry method, it is left intact during drying. The parchment is the hull that envelops the coffee bean.

Seed

The coffee seed or bean is made up of an outer 'silver skin,' a seed (endosperm) and an embryo (center). The silver skin is the outer layer of the seed. Generally, some of the silver skin remains on the bean before roasting, and some come off during coffee roasting. You can usually find some evidence of silver skin in your coffee beans after grinding; it is a sign of quality beans.

The seed is the principal part of the fruit. The chemical content of the endosperm determines the flavor and aroma of roasted coffee. Some of the compounds found in it are caffeine, proteins, minerals, and oils. The innermost part of the seed consists of the embryo, or what would become a new coffee plant should it germinate.

Coffee cherries drying in the sun (part of the natural processing method)

BEAN VARIETIES

There are multiple varieties within the Arabica species of plants, and they are not the only species either! We discuss these two in detail because they are the most common worldwide. Bear in mind that there are other species.

Regarded as the superior bean, Arabica produces smooth, rich, aromatic coffee. Arabica has a higher acidity which gives it the characteristic flavor profile that sets it apart from other varieties. These beans grow best in tropical regions with temperate weather, plenty of humidity and rain. Conditions should not be too hot or too cold, which is why they are often produced at higher altitudes.

The best quality beans are grown in the shade of larger trees, with reduced sun exposure to allow a full ripening process. Growing on hillsides means that the only way to pick the berries is by hand. Hand picking anticipates that only the best berries will be collected. Also, the berries must be picked regularly. They must not be allowed to become over-ripe. This makes Arabica beans costlier to produce, and it also helps to maintain quality.

Robusta, on the other hand, is a hardier type of coffee which is suited for growing in tougher conditions like full sun. It is easier to grow and is less vulnerable to pests and the weather as it is more drought hardy than

Arabica. Robusta plants produce a much higher yield per plant than Arabica. This variety produces a stronger, more full-bodied flavor which also contains more caffeine. It is often grown in flat areas, not on hillsides or in the shade, allowing for the berries to be strip picked mechanically.

All of these elements make Robusta the cheaper variety to produce, and it is the low price that many instant coffee producers find attractive when they are cost engineering their coffee products. Still, many coffee roasters mix Robusta into their blends to strengthen the profile of their coffee. It is quite hard to find a pure Robusta blend.

Arabica beans are slightly elongated compared to the Robusta bean which is more rounded.

HARVESTING

Coffee beans are harvested once per year during the dry season in lower-altitude and sub-tropical regions. Equatorial regions may be able to harvest beans continually throughout the year.

The Baristas Ultimate Guide to Coffee

COFFEA ARABICA.—Linn.— Blanco.—DC.

Coffee berries on a branch, ripe and unripe berries usually present at the same time.

- Hand-picked coffee: the berries on the branch are rarely all ripe at the same time. Generally, a single branch will contain berries at various stages of development. Workers walk through the plantation carrying baskets and select only the ripe berries. In some regions, where coffee plantations sit on steep hill sides, this is the only possible way to pick the beans.
- Mechanical shaker: Another method used to collect only ripe berries is to pass a mechanical shaker over through the plantation. This machine shakes the coffee shrubs enough so that any mature berries fall off the branch and any green berries stay on. The ripe berries fall into collection trays and the mechanical shaker returns in a week or so for another pass through the crops. This is only

possible in certain regions, landscape permitting.
- Stripping: Simply put, all the berries on a branch will be stripped off at once. Collecting ripe and unripe berries together. This method is common in regions where the harvest season is clearly defined so that most of the berries on the branch will ripen at the same time (more or less).

PROCESSING

Once harvested, coffee berries must be processed to remove the beans from the fruit. Harvesting and processing methods have developed strictly depending on the region's climate and technological conditions. Just as the environment affects the beans qualities, so does the processing after harvesting.

Some aspects are common to all methods; berries are sorted and cleaned, over-ripe, or damaged berries are removed and any other unwanted debris like twigs, soil or leaves are also removed.

Natural/Dry Processing

The ripe berries are spread out in the sun in broad patios. They are hand raked to ensure even drying until they look like nuts. Depending on the weather conditions, it might take up to 4 weeks before the berries are ready for the next step. During the drying process, sugars in the berry may ferment and absorb into the bean, creating a typical natural processed taste and a heavier body.

The sun-dried berries are taken to a mill where they are mechanically hulled, removing all the skin and mucilage at once. The beans are then sorted, graded, and bagged.

The natural process is used to develop a fruity and acidic taste and is widely employed in African countries where water may be in shorter supply.

Coffee being sorted and cleaned by hand in African coffee production

Wet/Washed Processing

The wet or washed process is considered to produce a better quality coffee, by preserving the beans' qualities and producing a more homogeneous batch of green coffee beans.

The berries are dropped into tanks full of flowing water, using screens to separate berries by size.

Next, they go into a pulping machine, which squeezes the bean (with parchment intact) out of the fruit. This process removes the outer skin and most of the fruit mucilage. The beans may be allowed to ferment for a period before being washed again to leave only the clean, green coffee beans.

After that, these beans are dried by laying out in the sun or by using a mechanical hot air dryer to produce what is called 'parchment' coffee beans (this just means they still have the parchment intact).

This process is mainly associated with Arabica coffee beans. It is a more expensive process that helps to achieve a cleaner taste and a more delicate and well-defined flavor.

Others

In Sumatra, they use a traditional method, which is somewhere between wet and dry processing. This method is characterized for helping the beans gain more earthy tones and making a full bodied coffee.

More recently another method has gained popularity in Central America, called the Honey Process, which combines techniques from the wet process (the beans are hulled before drying) and from a natural process (the hulled beans are allowed to dry in the sun with some of the mucilage still present). This method produces a sweeter coffee bean since it has allowed for some of the sugars from the cherry to remain.

GRADING

Both wet and dry processed green beans are sorted and graded before going on sale. The parchment is mechanically removed, and the beans pass through some cleaning cycles, screening and sorting by size, weight, and color (often using electronic methods that can detect irregularities), leading to a final grading that will help the buyers choose their beans.

There isn't an internationally recognized system, and so it varies around the world. Coffee beans are classified by the number of defects per kilo (defects like insect damage, broken or chipped beans, and remaining parchment).

The top grade without defects (could be less than 3% defects) will be sold for the highest price. Those interested in top grade beans will market them as Speciality or Premium coffee and will likely be sold on as beans (as opposed to ready ground).

Beans with more defects demand a lower price and usually remain for national consumption in the country where it is produced and are also used for making instant coffee. It is worth noting that these grading systems only look at the physical aspects of the beans and never consider the flavor.

COFFEE REGIONS

Coffee cultivation is concentrated in areas roughly bounded by the Tropics of Cancer and Capricorn. These growing regions typically offer moderate sunshine and rain and steady temperatures of around 20°C (68°F), not to forget to mention the rich soil. Each region tends to generate a different flavor profile, and you may need to be able to hone your tasting skills to be able to recognize these.

The flavor and quality of your Espresso will depend greatly on the bean. When you embark on your journey to finding your favorite Espresso, it is best to start with single origin beans. It is entirely possible that each coffee farm or plantation in the world will produce a slightly different taste profile. Aspects like the weather, soil, amounts of sunlight and water, use of artificial or natural fertilizers can all affect the flavor.

Just like wine, coffees taste is affected by its growing conditions. But that's just half the story. The way coffee is processed after harvest is dependent on regional geography. Areas with plenty of water will wash the beans while arid regions will dry them in the sun, adding another layer to the reasons why the region affects the flavor.

To break it down, we generalize each region into a profile. Become familiar with these profiles, and you will be able to discern a Kenyan bean from a Peruvian one.

CENTRAL AMERICA

The Central America region stretches from Veracruz, South Mexico to Guatemala, Honduras, and Costa Rica. This is a vast area that contains many micro climates. How can we clump it all together? Well, there is one thing that the area has in common, and that is this; this area is mountainous, and the land is rich in the volcanic soil!

Mostly, small landholders work to produce Arabica beans. Plentiful rainfall ensures the plants have enough water naturally, and for the most part, plantations are found in the shade of other trees, a traditional method of coffee farming that does not require intense fertilization. This method is the best for the environment because it protects the land and allows birds and animals to cohabit the land while the farmers are working.

The wet process is used for bean processing in this region. The beans can be generalized as acidic, fruity, smooth, and sugar-like. Words like chocolate and butter, pear and vanilla are also often used to describe coffee from this area. It is also considered well rounded and balanced.

An example of a coffee plantation in the shade of the rainforest, typical to Central America

COLOMBIA

Possibly the most famous country for producing coffee, this country is divided by the Andes mountain range, with a coast on the Pacific Ocean and another on the Caribbean sea. While most coffee production in Colombia is still in the hands of small landholders, technology use has increased year on year.

Many of the coffee plantations are on steep sides of mountains, and mechanized picking is not available. However the region has adopted the methodology of sun cultivation, whereby the coffee plantation is not growing in the shade of other trees, rather it is growing in the full sun to induce faster and fuller crops.

Colombian coffee is medium bodied, clean, containing mild acidity, strong caramel tones, with an intense aroma; A well-rounded coffee.

Coffee picking in Colombia, 1880's

BRAZIL

Brazil is the world's largest producer of Arabica coffee. This country does not specialize in just one type of coffee; they produce a lot of Robusta as well. To produce so much coffee, a lot of lands is needed. Vast areas of land that used to be grassland or rainforest are now used for coffee.

This is modern day, conventional mass farming of coffee. You will find the use of both dry and washed processing methods as well as automated strip picking machines. Use of this process also means that the picked cherries are not all ripe but a mix of green and ripe cherries, so another process of sorting (also mechanized) is required.

The coffee from Brazil can be described as sweet and nutty, low in acidity, creamy and chocolatey.

Coffee is grown in full sun with use of modern industrial farming technology

ETHIOPIA

Ethiopia has a great reputation for producing excellent beans. There is a wealth of experience in processing coffee the natural way, drying it on open patios to achieve a bright and fruity full bodied coffee.

Ethiopian coffee beans getting dried (part of the natural processing method)

INDONESIA

Coffee from Java is mostly Arabica with a wet process preparation. It is grown on the sides of volcanoes at around 1400 meters above sea level. A good Java coffee exhibits a relatively heavy body though lighter than some others from the wider region; it is not very acidic.

A fine Java coffee has a low-toned richness that is typical of Indonesian and New Guinea coffees, but with a full body that is clean and thick, and a medium acidity along with earthy qualities. These coffees are less earthy than Sumatran coffee and often contain a slightly spicy or smoky twist. The largest and best coffee producers in Java are plantations that were established by the Dutch East India Company.

Coffee from Sumatra is traditionally processed using a method called Giling Basah. This method tends to create herbaceous, spicy, mushroomy and earthy notes. Usually distinguished by their full body and low acidity, Sumatran coffees are known for providing a rich, satisfying flavor. It can often exhibit intense tones of chocolate and licorice.

ESPRESSO BEANS

In a later chapter, we'll discuss how Espresso is different from other brewing methods. You may have noticed on coffee packaging; 'for Espresso machine,' 'Espresso roast,' or 'Espresso blend.' Each refers to a different aspect of the coffee as we will discover in later chapters. For now, let's focus on what's meant when you see 'Espresso blend.'

So what is an 'Espresso blend'?

An Espresso blend is a carefully selected blend of coffee beans that will create a balanced Espresso.

The high-pressure method used for Espresso extracts aromatics from the coffee beans. Each variety of bean possesses both pleasant and unpleasant elements. For example, Robusta beans can be very astringent (unpleasantly so) which makes is highly unsuitable for Espresso. Many Espresso blends contain small amounts of Robusta, commonly used to improve the crema and add body to Arabica beans.

An Espresso blend is typically made using different coffee beans, carefully selected for this particular extraction method. Sometimes it could be made from two to three single origins, other times as many as 15 single origin beans are blended. Think of it like comparing a symphony to a solo act; neither is better or worse, and each must be judged accordingly.

You may have heard that a blend of 100% Arabica is superior to a blend using Robusta - that is a myth. A well-made blend using Robusta can be just as good as or better than a blend with only Arabica beans. The quality of the blend depends on the beans, the blend selected, and the roasting process.

The benefit of using a blend is to ensure the same flavor profile over time. Remember that coffee is highly affected by environmental conditions, such as rain or the sun. Imagine that the normally dry season for drying beans in Ethiopia is suddenly cloudy this year, increasing the time it takes to dry the beans would certainly affect their taste after roasting. By using blends of beans from many different countries, you can swap or change amounts of each type of bean to achieve a consistent flavor profile over long periods of time.

A professionally crafted blend will take into account many aspects, such as; compatibility, complementary nature and constancy over time. It is important each bean contains components that are compatible with those of the other beans. They should also complement each other, filling in for what the other lacks. Plus, roasters look for beans that come from stable sources and regions where quality standards are adhered to consistently.

A typical Italian Espresso blend contains up to 60% Arabica beans of high quality to provide a sound basis for the Espresso blend. 20-30% Robusta beans are used to give the Espresso a quality crema and add strength, especially important when creating milk based drinks. The last 10-20% of the blend is made up of top grade high-quality Arabica beans especially selected to give the combination it's 'signature' flavor profile.

CAFFEINE

Caffeine, in its chemical form, is a white odourless and bitter tasting substance. It is found naturally in many plant species like tea and coffee. The amount of caffeine in your coffee depends on the water to coffee ratio, the blend of beans (Robusta contains more than Arabica) and the roast (darker roasts provide a little less).

Caffeine consumption is beneficial to your health (in moderation, as with all things). Some of the positive effects are increased concentration, attention, and memory. To consume a dangerous amount of caffeine from coffee, you would need to drink 100 Espressos one after another.

Depending on your physical makeup, your build, weight, age, etc., you will react to it in your way. Consuming too much caffeine may cause you to stay awake for longer, lose appetite, have headaches, feel anxious or even give you temporary shakiness.

DECAFFEINATION

Decaffeinated beans contain less than 0.1% caffeine. There are three ways to remove the caffeine. These are the Solvent method, Swiss Water method and CO2 method. What distinguishes these methods is the substance used for extraction. Why should you care? You should at least know what happened to your beans on their way to your cup.

Traditional Solvent based method of extracting caffeine uses a chemical solvent, which is not entirely removed from the beans after processing. That means you include an additional chemical into your cup of coffee which may affect the taste (and your health).

The Swiss Water method uses water as the solvent to decaffeinate coffee, it was originally developed in Switzerland in the 1980s and is now used commercially under the trademark "Swiss Water Process." You can immerse green coffee beans in water to extract their caffeine, but this will also extract all the oils which give it the characteristic flavors. The Swiss Water method uses water that is already infused with coffee oils, so the only part that gets removed from the beans is the caffeine. The water used is called green coffee extract. It is created using a separate batch of green coffee beans, which are immersed in water and then discarded. The water is then filtered to remove only the caffeine from it. A fresh batch of green coffee beans is then immersed in this coffee water which removes caffeine but retains other components. This process can remove caffeine up to 99.9% by mass.

The CO2 method uses Carbon Dioxide. The beans are soaked in water until doubled in size, and the caffeine is dissolved in the water. Beans enter a 20-meter tall chamber at the top and slowly travel down the chamber in which liquid carbon dioxide and water help to extract the caffeine while leaving the rest of the coffee properties untouched. This fluid/gas solvent process requires much less water, so it is considered a greener method of producing decaf.

INSTANT COFFEE

'How easy it is now to get a rich, full-bodied cup of coffee. Just put a teaspoonful of Nescafe in a cup and add piping hot water. That's all! Thrifty, too! You make the exact amount you want—there's never any waste!' - Nescafe advert from 1889

Borden advert from 1880's, clearly did not have as much success as Nescafe.

Instant coffee has a terrible reputation amongst coffee lovers. However, it should be considered as a super practical way to enjoy coffee. For me, it is a last resort, I admit! It comes into its own for very specific uses and should not be written off entirely. It usually comes in glass jars, tins, and single serving sachets, and it is a soluble powder or granules that when mixed with hot water or milk makes coffee.

Two methods are used today to produce it. They are called spray drying or freeze drying. An industrial sized coffee machine brews the coffee (using low grade beans most commonly), then the water gets evaporated to leave behind only coffee particles. With the spray drying method, the brew gets sprayed into a hot air chamber where the water just evaporates and is removed in the air.

Freeze drying utilizes a process called sublimation. Just as before, a huge vat of coffee gets brewed.

The coffee is then frozen, then through applying massive amounts of pressure on the coffee ice, the water disappears (into vapor), and as if by magic only the coffee particles are left.

In the UK, over three-quarters of all coffee consumed is instant! People love the ease and convenience of instant coffee. You control the strength by the amount of powder that you use. It is also popular in baking. After reading this book, you will realize that it can be just as easy to enjoy freshly brewed coffee at home.

PART THREE

THE ROAST

ART OF ROASTING

I have measured out my life with coffee spoons - T.S. Eliot (poet)

Coffee roasting could be considered an art. On the surface, it is a very simple process; add dry heat to the green beans to release the flavour. In truth, however, coffee beans are like treasure chests that require a very special key to unlock the right flavours.

Washed and dried green coffee is a lot like any other dry bean. It can be stored for a long time yet remain fresh and aromatic after it is roasted or cooked. To make our dried green coffee ready for brewing, we must roast it. Without roasting, a beverage made from the green coffee bean would be bitter and extremely acidic.

The simple act of roasting coffee is still done at home in many coffee producing countries - literally from farm to cup for many coffee producers. This is because it is just as simple as toasting the beans in a skillet. However to achieve a well-balanced and consistent roast the coffee beans require a very well balanced machine that will heat evenly then cool properly.

Find some additional resources on our blog at www.boldbarista.com to help you along your journey of coffee discovery

ROASTING PROCESS

Roasting is a critical stage in coffee production. It is a stage that takes place in the country of consumption. Getting as close as possible to the roaster is how you will ensure you get the freshest brew.

During the roasting process, the beans change dramatically. The sugars in the beans more than anything else transform into hundreds of ephemeral aromatic substances, some of which get trapped in the fiber and oil.

Not the setup you want to be using, but goes to show it doesn't take much to roast your beans at home.

Heat increases the pressure inside the beans and forces out any water. As the beans absorb heat, the color gradually changes to yellow, and then to increasingly darker shades of brown. At this point, they may release a bit of a grassy smell. Soon, the beans start to steam as their internal temperature rises and begins to evaporate water content held inside. The coffee beans must be in constant motion to prevent scorching or uneven roasting. Drum roasters rotate while air roasters have arms that turn the coffee.

During the later stages of roasting, oils appear on the surface of the bean. The roast will continue to darken until it is removed from the heat source. Most roasters use a combination of bean mass temperature, smell, color, and sound to monitor the roasting process. The beans make a cracking sound (much like popcorn when it pops, but quieter) once when the inside temperature of the bean reaches about 200°C (392°F) (called the first crack). A second crack happens when the inside temperature of the beans reaches about 224°C (435°F). Some of the starch in the beans changes to sugars, some of which are transformed into carbon dioxide, and others are caramelized into the complex flavor that makes good coffee.

Freshly roasted coffee releases gasses, and the typical aroma fills the air. At the end of roasting, beans can be about 20% lighter in weight and up to twice as large as green beans. The heating process releases coffee oils - the essence of the drink in your cup. The roasting process frees and exposes these substances to oxygen. Once roasted, coffee should be consumed within two to three weeks. Oxidization can is an effect that affects the roasted beans as well as the brewed coffee!

The intricacies of coffee can only be revealed through careful preparation and great care from start to finish.

Green coffee beans go into the hopper, and when the temperature is right, they are fed into the roasting drum. The heat is carefully programmed, and typical commercial roasters will do a batch in 8-20 minutes. The roasted beans then drop into the grate where a pair of rakes moves the beans around to assist in cooling and to allow the beans to degas evenly. Roasted beans will continue to release gasses (like carbon dioxide) for about a month after roasting.

PACKING AND STORING

Green coffee beans will maintain their freshness for up to two years. Roasted beans can be considered as 'best before' since they will not go off in the way milk or fruit do. After roasting, beans require about a week to properly degas. This process allows the beans to stabilize chemically. The optimal flavor you can get from roasted beans comes between 5-20 days after roasting. Roasted beans will go off and become rancid if they are not stored properly.

The most common types of packaging for coffee today are paper and foil packs. Paper bags (sometimes with a small window) offer the least amount of protection and the shortest shelf life. You may find these from artisan roasters who roast and sell in small batches.

Foil material is an effective barrier against light, oxygen, and moisture and is the preferred choice of many coffee roasters. Coffee is unique in that it needs to be completely protected from oxygen while at the same time it gives off relatively large volumes of carbon dioxide (CO_2). You might notice that some foil packs contain a small valve. This one-way valve prevents oxygen from entering while CO_2 is allowed to escape. Coffee packaged this way will store for longer. Once opened and exposed to oxygen, you should consume it within a week.

Another technique used by the big roasters is to blast a shot of nitrogen into the packs before sealing. Using nitrogen is proven to maintain optimal freshness for longer. Supermarkets usually stock ground coffee which has been sealed with nitrogen and thus has a much longer shelf life.

I have found some brands which maintain the 'freshly roasted' taste and much more that just feel stale. What I mean is that, although it still tastes like coffee, it is missing most of the lovely notes and nuances of flavor that you find in freshly roasted beans. The type of coffee we buy in most supermarkets is almost entirely flat and dull.

The best way to keep roasted beans fresh is to keep away the elements that damage the flavour. Moisture, heat, light and other environmental factors. You should hold it in the original packaging, placing it into an airtight container. There is no need to keep it refrigerated!

ROASTING YOUR OWN

For most of us, buying green coffee beans is out of the question. With online shopping becoming so accessible, it is possible to buy green beans and roast your coffee at home. Additionally, you can even purchase home roasting machines that make the job all the more fun.

Buying roasted coffee beans from the supermarket you might be used to seeing a 'strength guide,' usually from 1-5 (5 commonly being the 'strongest').

Coffee strength is something you can change just by adding more or less coffee to your brew (we have all tasted weak watery coffee, it has nothing to do with the 'strength' of the roast). Many times what the 'strength guide' on the packaging refers to is the type of roast given to the beans, 1 being the lightest roast, and 5 being the darkest.

CLASSIFYING

Coffee beans change color during roasting. You can think of the image below as a general 'roast color' guide. Expert roasters look out for other signs of roast level as well; they listen for audio cues, they smell the aroma while roasting, they control the temperature and time in the roasting equipment, and they keep a close eye on the color.

The differences between roast profiles can be summarized as follows. Lightly roasted coffee maintains more of its acidity and 'bean' taste, bright and light. As the beans roast, the sweetness and bitterness begin to develop. Acidity is lost as bitterness grows. Dark roast beans contain caramel, and chocolate notes with fewer of the beans own characteristics. A very dark roast will have lost all of the beans characteristics and impart only the roasted flavor notes.

Light Roast; At 'first crack' the steam becomes fragrant. The color is light brown to golden. Sugar, s begin to caramelize, and bitterness has not yet developed. Brewing this roast creates sharp and complex acidity, notes of roasted grains. The beans own characteristics will come through strongly.

Medium Roast; Somewhere between the first and second crack, the color is medium to dark brown. This roast allows for more of the beans characteristics to come through than a darker roast, yet still, allows a moderate level of sweetness and bitterness to develop.

Dark Roast; The sugars continue to caramelize well after the second crack, the beans color turns dark brown and becomes shiny as the oils are pushed onto the surface. Visually very different to

Lighter roasts which look dull, dark roasted beans are shiny and oily. At this point, the beans original flavors cannot be readily distinguished. The flavors are caramels and bittersweet; the acidity is all gone.

Charcoal - you won't want to drink that! Overly roasted beans are not consumable. These are beans that may have been roasted for too long or at very high temperature. The bean will become ash and carbon, all the soluble substances burnt off.

You may have heard of 'burnt' coffee before, that refers to when too much heat is used during brewing. Sometimes Espresso machines fall out of calibration, and the water temperature may increase a few degrees or the time to pour the Espresso may take a few extra seconds. Those small changes will make an Espresso that is 'burnt,' you will notice a very dark crema and little aroma. It would taste overly bitter.

It is easy to get caught up in a name, whether you prefer 'city' or 'vienna' or 'cinammon' roast - it varies so much. Your local roaster will have, their names for their signature roasts. When you understand the concept behind the name, then you can look beyond it. Find out what your local roaster has on offer and question why they choose that particular roast profile...

Each bean variety has it's own flavor, and each region brings its own geographical variances. So too does each roast profile impart it's own characteristics to the bean. Acidity diminishes as sweetness and bitterness develop through roasting. A very dark roast will eliminate most of the beans own profile and leave only the flavors developed through roasting.

THE ESPRESSO ROAST

In a later chapter, we explore how we brew Espresso. The high-pressure method extracts much more from the coffee beans, so beans are roasted to a particular set of specifications designed specifically for this mode of preparation.

Espresso is a drink originating in Italy. This particular drink has been shaped, over many years, by the tastes of a single nation. In Italy, the more commonly found coffee roasts are the darker ones. A dark roast with very little flavor coming from the bean itself... Usually, an Italian Espresso is quite chocolatey, bitter and flat, with none of the higher notes and with no acidity. When you see something labeled 'Espresso Roast' you can expect it to be a darker roast.

As Espresso has increased in popularity outside of continental Europe, it has also evolved to suit the tastes of locals in other regions. Espresso in the UK is lighter and brighter, more acidic, less bitter than in the continent. In the US you will find a difference between east and west coast. Espresso on the west coast will contain lighter roasted beans, and the east coast will contain darker roasts.

Keep in mind that these terms are not protected in any way and vary widely around the globe. For example, recently I found coffee at local roasters being packaged as 'Espresso Roast' and 'Filter Roast,' but after questioning, I discovered that both used the same roast profile: they were only ground differently. So what they 'meant' to say was 'Espresso Grind' and 'Filter Grind'…

PART FOUR

THE GRIND

WHAT IS IT?

Science may never come up with a better office communication system than the coffee break. -Earl Wilson (journalist)

You telling me there is a whole section of the book about grinding? Yes, we grind the coffee beans so that we can extract all the right stuff with greater ease. In the past, crushing beans in a mortar and pestle proved an easy way to improve the brewing time and extraction. This significant development leads to the creation of Turkish coffee - which is still served today.

It also opened up a new challenge - how to separate the coffee from the used grounds! In this chapter we look at:
- The different aspects of each grind profile.
- How each grind profile is appropriate for each method of brewing.
- What is 'extraction.'
- How the grind affects extraction.

Coffee aficionados all agree that grinding your beans yourself is fundamental to getting the best tasting coffee at home. You could even say that the grinder is more important than the brewing method!

As I mentioned earlier, I started drinking coffee quite late, and as I learned more about the subject, I quickly started brewing at home (initially with the pre-ground coffee I could buy at my local supermarket). I soon began researching and learning all I could. I found out what freshly roasted and just ground coffee could taste like, and it was like 'whoa, where did that come from!'

We already know that we have to mix coffee with hot water to extract the flavor. If you took the whole bean, it would just take ages to get all the taste out. So we have to make it easier for the water to extract the goodness from the coffee beans, we have to break it up. A ground bean allows a larger surface area to be covered by the water, so a quicker extraction of coffee goodness is possible.

No surprise then that smaller particles also shorten the time it takes for the hot water to act on extracting oils and flavor from the coffee.

There are some inherent factors in the beans that will affect the grinding process. For example, if the beans contain too much moisture they will produce a poor grind with inconsistently sized particles. Darker roasts, beans that have been roasted for longer, are more brittle and tend to produce more fine powdery particles within the grind. Same can be said for older beans that have been in storage for a longer time. Lighter roasts, produce more consistent results and create fewer of the fine powdery particles.

Wall mounted coffee grinders in use until the 20th century.

TYPES

When is each grind size appropriate? In general, coarser grinds will need more time in contact with water. The amount of time decreases as the grind gets finer. Use this as a guide and refer to the brewing methods chapter for more details on each brewing device.

Coarse - distinguished by particles that look like grains of sea salt. It's chunky, pieces of coffee beans, you can easily recognize the individual pieces. Cold brewing methods require an extra coarse grind - as it is going to brew for over 12 hours, larger granules are okay for that brewing process. Use coarse ground coffee in a cafetière (French press) or with the Eva Solo. Any brewing method that uses mesh filters is better suited for coarser granules since mesh filters allow smaller particles to pass through.

Medium - feels like sand or sugar, you can still see the individual particles. It's gritty and loose to allow water to absorb the soluble particles more quickly and particles are large enough that they will not clog the filter. Use medium ground coffee in filter coffee machines and most paper filter methods of brewing (like V60 and Chemex).

Fine - feel smooth to the touch, and tough to see individual particles. It packs together with ease. Sometimes just referred to as Espresso coffee. Use it for pressure brewing methods like the Aeropress, Rok, a moka pot and all Espresso machines.

Turkish - feels like powder and no grains should be visible. Looks and feels like flour, packs, and clumps together easily. Only used with a cezve or ibrik and never for an Espresso (machines will clog or worse, you could cause a dangerous burst of hot water).

FILTERS

Each grind profile is suited to different filtering methods. There are various kinds of filters, made of natural and synthetic materials. You can find reusable as well as disposable filters, read on to learn more about each kind.

Paper filters come in natural or bleached variations. Natural filters can be brown and may have a strong papery smell. Also, even after rinsing, the natural filter can give off a cardboard like a scent that will become absorbed by the brew. Bleached filters are white and have little to no smell, because of the bleaching process. These are widely used in cafes. Some may be more sensitive to the paper smell imparted by some brands of natural filters. The paper filter also allows for easier cleanup, with little to no sediment.

Regarding taste, paper filters will allow fewer oils to pass through into the cup, helping to highlight the floral and sweet notes of a lighter roast. At the same time, a paper filter can also contribute to
silence some of the rich, dark chocolate flavors of a roast. This can also cause a loss of body and robustness, which are popular characteristics of a press pot, so this can factor into your general preference.

Metal filters will allow flavor carrying oils to pass through the filter into the cup. Metal filters are not so fine as paper to catch all the sediment. This can create an overall grittiness, but you will also experience a lot of flavor nuances that would otherwise be removed by the paper filter. Metal filters are reusable and usually require a quick rinse under running water.

Cloth filters are reusable but lack the ease of use that you get with a disposable paper filter. A cloth filter can offer the best aspects of paper and metal filters. They allow for oils to pass through without

The sediment. Keep in mind that cloth filters come with a bit of maintenance. Not only do they need to be cleaned after each use and they must be stored in either a cup of water or a plastic bag in the refrigerator. If you ensure proper maintenance, a cloth filter can last roughly three to six months.

The important thing is to find something that works best for you and your preferred coffee.

AIDING EXTRACTION

Extraction only refers to how much flavor has been taken from the coffee grounds that were used. The level of extraction is also factored in by how much time water is left within the bed of coffee grinds. Thus, if water is held too long, then over-extraction will occur, while water that is not held long enough can create under-extraction.

Also, keep in mind that grind size and turbulence can also create the differences in extraction. Besides, there is a definite difference between coffee that is merely bitter or sour for its own sake or a very clear case of a poorly extracted coffee.

- An unbalanced flavor that is bitter indicates that the coffee is over-extracted.
- An unbalanced flavor, highly acidic and sour finish indicates that the coffee is under-ex- tracked.
- A well balanced flavor with acidity, sweetness, and bitterness in line with the type of coffee used shows a well-extracted coffee

Grind
- Coarse for steeped coffee.
- Medium for filter coffee.
- Fine for Espresso.

Water to Coffee Ratio
- Typically, coffee grounds are matched with the appropriate dose of water. A quality cup of coffee requires 10g of coffee per 100g of water.
- For a single Espresso, 7-10g of coffee is used (in 25ml water).
- For a double Espresso, 14-18g of coffee is used (in 50ml water).

Brew Time

When water is in contact with the coffee, it will begin to dissolve at a specific rate. Thus, keep mind that:

- Filter Coffee (1 liter or more) takes 4-6 minutes.
- Single cup filter, approximately 1-3 minutes.
- Espresso, approximately 20-30 seconds.

Water Temperature

Like the length of time, you want to ensure that you are drawing out the desired flavors, which can be aided by heat. As a general rule, the temperature should range between 92-96°C (197-206°F).

Turbulence

In coffee, we say 'turbulence' to refer to the motion of the coffee grounds in water. We know that the amount of time the coffee is in contact with the water directly affects the levels of extraction. Turbulence or movement also plays a part. When you pour water on coffee grounds, you can give it a stir to improve extraction by separating the coffee grounds, allowing water to flow all around each particle.

GRIND IT GOOD

A good grinder has to produce even results; you don't want inconsistency for any brewing method you use. Metal Blade 'grinders' are available quite cheaply and will do the job ok for some types of brewing (certainly not recommended for Espresso). The blades revolve at high speed to crash into the beans and chop repeatedly breaking apart and disintegrating the beans. The high speed involved generates heat (which can damage the beans and impair the taste). But more importantly, you can't control the grind size precisely enough for Espresso. You can leave the beans in the grinder for longer, but you can never achieve a consistent enough grind for great Espresso.

Ideally, you want to look for what is known as a burr grinder. It is a simple mechanism that involves two rotating surfaces that crush the beans. You can control the distance between the two surfaces, a larger distance creates a coarser grind, and a smaller distance produces a finer grind. This mechanism is common, think of salt and pepper mills! Grinders vary widely in price and ease of use. Stainless steel mechanisms are the best and most reliable over longer periods of time. This type of grinder is more expensive and works similarly to professional large-scale mills that crush the coffee into the desired size.

Commercial grinders are suitable for constant daily use. Home grinders usually mirror the above and have smaller capacities. A great grinder will give you full control of the grind size and be able to set the dosing to the exact amount you need for your machine.

What we would expect is for it to produce a consistent and good quality grind for home use. And as I stated before, grinding at home just before you brew using ANY home grinder is better than buying pre-ground coffee. Even on a restricted budget, you can find a suitable grinder. Buying freshly roasted coffee beans and grinding them to order - even with a blade grinder - is better than keeping an open packet of pre-ground coffee.

Hand grinders aren't as noisy as electric grinders, which can be very loud. Every time you are preparing a coffee, you grind just what you need. Manual grinders are easy to use and very easy to clean up after. Depending on the design that you get, you may find that manual grinders can be fiddly, requiring re-assembly for each use. However maintenance is minimal and there is little chance of breakdowns.

A good hand grinder will use burrs made of 100% steel or ceramic, it should feel solid to provide
good consistency. You should be able to quickly and comfortably grind a medium or coarse for your
cafetière or drip machine.

A few manual grinders can make a fine enough powder for Espresso. Also most hand grinders cannot do a consistent enough grind for Espresso machines. Grinding by hand is too slow when grinding for Espressos. If you are preparing coffee for yourself, or using drip or steep methods, then a manual grinder will do the job just fine.

Electric blade grinder
You need to grind and you are on a budget, consider a blade grinder. These are available very cheaply, and in many designs. Personally, I suggest you save up for a good mill instead. Electric grinders will apply some heat to the beans, which could damage the taste. And while they are fine for drip and cafetière, you will not achieve a really consistent grind for Espresso.

Electric burr grinder
This is the type of grinder you would expect at a cafe or at a roaster. Burr grinders are great for achieving consistency, shot after shot. Espresso requires a lot of fine grinding, which is best achieved with an electric grinder. Even if you are just making for yourself, you will save so much time and hassle by choosing electric over manual.

Remember to look out for a 100% steel mechanism. You may go for something with many additional features like electric timers and auto adjustments of grind. Some models can be programmed with the right dose, so that you can grind the exact amount each time. Another important thing to consider is how easy is it to clean! Cleaning is important, as leftover residual pieces of ground coffee will stale over time and may end up tainting the freshly ground coffee.

THE ESPRESSO GRIND

As brewing Espresso is different from other brewing methods, it requires a specific type of grind.

Espresso grind is fine, yet it never aims to have all the particles of the same size. There should be specks of dust and particles up to 1mm in length. The consistency is of much greater importance when using an Espresso machine than with any other brew method. With Espresso, you are aiming at getting hot pressured water through 7 grams of coffee to produce exactly 25 ml in 25 seconds!

That is why the grind is so important.

THE BARISTAS ROLE

For a great Espresso, we need the correct amount of coffee grounds (the dose) to be at the right consistency or 'grind.' Placing too much coffee in the basket will lead to a longer extraction time and a heavier, stronger Espresso. Not enough coffee in the basket and you will get a quicker brew, but without the strength you expect.

As a Barista you must be able to recognize when the dose is correct for your piece of equipment and setup. Grinders may come with dosing features, or you may use a scale. A traditional shot of Espresso uses 7 grams of coffee, while a double or strong Espresso requires 14 grams. The ideal 'extraction time' should be no less than 20 seconds and never more than 30 seconds.

The modern day grinder/dispenser you see in coffee shops must also consistently dose the exact preprogrammed amount, working in conditions of variable and changing temperature and humidity. They are crafted to work day in and day out, requiring minimal maintenance and adjustments. A home grinder should do the same on a domestic basis. The best machine will require little manual adjustment to achieve great results.

You may adjust the grind (either coarser or finer) so that the timing of your Espresso is the ideal extraction time of 20-30 seconds.

This level of adjustment is very fine! Finer grounds will slow the machine down while coarser grounds will speed it up. Your coffee grinder may only have only a few built in settings, and it may not be able to adjust the grind to this level. However, if you are using a more professional grinder, it should allow you to adjust the grinding step by step. These micro adjustments to the grind will alter the extraction time just one second at a time. Patience is certainly a virtue!

As a Barista you must be aware of the 'ideal extraction time,' and you must monitor it, to ensure each of your Espressos stays within the ideal range. If your Espresso is falling outside the range, try to investigate why. Remember that coffee beans are highly sensitive to temperature and humidity levels, these factors influence how well the beans grind. Also, consider the condition of the actual grinder, and whether it is in need of maintenance or simply needs readjustment.

PART FIVE
TASTING

CUPPING

Coffee cupping is a tasting technique used in the industry to evaluate coffee on various aspects of aroma and flavor profile. It is a simple technique that requires very basic equipment so anyone can do it. Farmers, dealers, and buyers can easily set up a cupping session to evaluate and compare their crops. Buyers use this technique to find out which beans will suit their blend, finding the traits and faults in the green beans and deciding how to roast and blend each one.

Essential cupping equipment: hot water and pouring kettle, spoons, glasses of water...

Master Tasters use the cupping technique when blending coffee. In the industry, the Master Taster of a roastery is responsible for blending coffee beans from different countries to maintain a consistent flavor batch after batch for their clients.

In a cupping session, you will find samples of the green, roasted, and ground coffee for each bean to be tasted. Buyers want to see the sample of green bean to inspect visual qualities. Light roasted beans are used for cupping since this will allow more of the bean's taste to come through. And the ground coffee is for brewing. There will be spoons and cups of hot water to rinse the spoons.

The first stage is visual inspection and to note the smell of the freshly ground coffee before adding water - that is referred to like the fragrance.

The freshly boiled water is added to the cups and left to brew for about two to three minutes untouched. Usually, a ratio of 5g to 100ml of hot water is used, and the roast used for cupping is always light. After adding the water, the coffee grounds will float to the surface and form a crust. To note the aroma, tasters use a spoon, placing their nose close to the cup, they push the spoon into the brewed coffee for the first time. This is referred to as breaking the crust.

After that, the grounds are scooped out or left to sink to the bottom of the cup. At this point, tasters may also scoop out any foam. Tasters use the spoon to take a couple of sips of coffee. Tasters slurp the spoonful of coffee forcefully so that air and coffee burst in and cover as much of the inside of their mouth as possible.

It is important to get the coffee onto all of the tongue and even the back of the throat. Two sips are required as a minimum before noting all the observations regarding the taste, acidity, body, and aftertaste. Taste is subjective, and tasters will often disagree. Coffee tasting should be fun, and it is not a competition to see who gets the most inventive or flowery description.

Industrial coffee roasters are focused on providing a consistent flavor profile for their customers, and cupping plays an important part in maintaining that quality. Most coffee out there is a blend,

Usually using beans from many countries, often mixing Arabica and Robusta varieties. Starbucks, Costa, Lavazza, Illy... they all use the same technique to maintain the flavor profile their customers are used to in their coffee blend.

TASTING EXERCISE

You can also use this method to discover the nuances of the different coffees available to you and to find out what your preferences are. You can set up a cupping session at home with coffee beans from various countries side-by-side to understand the little differences between coffee growing regions. Start with freshly ground single origin coffee beans.

Aroma of the dry ground coffee (the fragrance)

Start by using your nose, the most powerful of your senses when it comes to flavor. How do the dry coffee grounds smell? You can use a clean spoon to move the grounds and release more aroma. Is the coffee smell fresh or stale? Over roasted or burnt? Under-roasted and perhaps grassy? Other words you may use at this stage are:

Sweet, Spicy, Toasty, Nutty, Malty, Carbone, Stale, Fresh

Aroma of the wet ground coffee (breaking the crust)

Now add some freshly boiled water onto the coffee. Allow it to sit for 2 minutes; the grounds will be floating at the top forming a 'crust.' Get your nose up close and use a clean spoon to 'break' the crust. Allow your nose to do the work. What do you sense? The sensation should be more intense than it was with the dry grounds. Note anything you sense. Some words you may use are:

Smooth, Fresh, Lively, Creamy, Sharp

Tasting

You could scoop out some of the ground coffee out of the cup, or if you see that it has sunk to the bottom, you can proceed to the tasting part. Using a clean spoon, fill it with coffee and give it a good healthy sip, allowing lots of air to rush in along with the coffee so that it covers the inside of your mouth and tongue. Careful not to burn yourself and remember that two sips are required. The first sip will prepare your taste buds and the second sip will be more accurate at finding flavors. Make a note of what you taste in each category (Acidity, Body, Taste and Aftertaste).

Acidity:
Nippy, Neutral, Soft, Tangy, Tart, Rough, Mild, Delicate, Smooth, Winey

Body:
Full, Rich, Fat, Thin

Taste/Depth:
Fruity, Winey, Buttery, Caramel, Chocolate, Blackcurrant, Woody, Grassy, Honey, Liquorice,
Malty, Nutty, Spicy

Aftertaste/Finish:
Sweet, Sour, Bitter, Sharp, Smooth, Full, Silky, Burnt, Dry

Coffee Tasting Notes

The following terms are frequently used during tastings. I hope these definitions will help you while you carry out your own coffee tasting sessions at home.

Sweetness:

Sugars are present in coffee, both in the fruit and in the bean. The roasting process diminishes a number of sugars, as these toast to form other compounds, some level of caramelisation may be present in the cup. Lighter roasts keep more of those sugars intact. Try a lightly roasted Costa Rican bean filter coffee!

Acidity:

Acidity is a pleasant sensation found naturally in coffee which also diminishes through roasting. The type of processing also affects the levels of acidity. Ethiopian coffee is famous for being highly acidic, resembling berries. Acidity in a coffee can give liveliness and freshness to the flavor.

Bitterness:

Inherent in coffee. In nature, bitterness alerts us to dangerous substances. Perhaps it is the plant's natural pest repellent! Robusta is noticeably more bitter than Arabica. Your coffee becomes more bitter as it cools down and you will find it also if you allow the water to extract for too long. You can train your brain that coffee bitterness is acceptable, and you can use sugar to make it more palatable.

Astringency:

Often confused with acidity, we tend to fight off astringency using milk and sugar. There is some substance in coffee that binds with the saliva glands in your mouth to give a sensation of dryness.
Your jaws may feel like they are closed up and you may feel a loss of sensation.

FRESHNESS

Remember, coffee is a delicate thing! Always use freshly roasted beans, never older than three months. Ensure you are getting your beans in a properly sealed bag. Grind only what you plan to use, and use immediately after grinding. Never store beans in the grinder hopper for longer than required. Beans should be stored in an airtight container, away from light and heat. Any moisture and extremes in temperature will diminish the freshness and the taste. There is no need to store coffee in the fridge!

After grinding, the coffee granules and coffee oils have come into contact with oxygen. Oxidization is like the taste and aroma of the beans decomposing. This means the oils may become rancid and makes a unpleasant substance. That coffee will be undrinkable.

And remember - over everything else, freshly roasted is a sign that your coffee will taste great.

PART SIX
MILK WATER SUGAR

MILK

Both hot and cold coffee drinks include milk as the main ingredient. Milk quality is affected by the environment the cows live in, the cows' diet and the weather. In the autumn cows are taken indoors and have a change in diet that affects the milk they produced.
For the best taste, you should opt for quality organic milk, with a good amount of fat to produce a great texture.

I find fat free or skimmed milk far too watery, and I enjoy the creaminess of semi-skimmed and whole fat milk when I drink a latte or cappuccino.

Perfectly prepared milk is silky smooth, velvety and sweet with an almond-like aroma. Drinks like Cappuccino and Latte require steamed or frothed milk. This velvety hot milk is an emulsion of air and milk. This thickening is due to the proteins in the milk, not the fat. The lipids in the milk help the emulsion stabilize, which is why the best Cappuccino and Latte milk is made using fresh whole milk.

Milk Alternatives
You can choose not to use cows' milk. Perhaps you are allergic to it, or just don't like the taste of cows' milk. Nowadays, you can find many alternatives like rice, oat, hemp, quinoa, or goats' milk. Go ahead and try out different combinations. Most coffee shops offer you the choice of soya milk as standard, and more often you will also find almond milk as an alternative.

Find the one that will take your coffee to the next level of awesome and avoid trying to find something that will replace the taste of cows' milk. If you want 'an alternative that tastes like milk' - you simply won't find it.

Sticks to cows' milk or find an appreciation for alternative milk's flavor. Almond and hazelnut are excellent choices for coffee!

Here are some alternatives that are available...

Camel - Not dissimilar to cow's milk, with added hints of nuts and smokiness. Across the Middle East and North and East Africa, camel milk is commonly used in cafes. Camel milk is rich in iron, with half the fat and up to five times the Vitamin C of cows' milk. It has a slightly salty undertone with an earthy taste. It is very refreshing and lighter than cow's milk. Plus it has loads of health benefits.

Coconut - There are two distinct products labeled as coconut milk. The more common is the tinned version, which is better suited for cooking as the fatty solids tend to separate. The other is packages similarly to other milk alternatives, in 1 liter packs and labeled as 'coconut milk drink.' It tastes distantly of coconut in a pleasant way. Watery and thin, it produces medium to big bubbles when steamed, so it is not a great alternative for coffees.

Goat - The taste of goats milk really divides opinion. Some people can't stomach it; others love it. However, it really varies depending on the brand. Shop around and try different brands if you want to take advantage of one of the healthiest options to cow milk. It foams nicely, although not as good as full-fat cows milk.

Nuts (Almond, cashew, hazelnut) - Nuts create a unique flavor that goes well with coffee, whether you use almonds, cashews or hazelnuts, it will bring a light taste of the nuts into your coffee. I'm talking about the homemade variety, made using a blender or juicer and raw nuts.
Homemade nut milk is superior to the mass produced stuff in taste and nutritional value. These general froth well and create a silky texture. I love nut milk with my coffee, both hot and cold.

Rice - Rice milk is neither nutritious nor does it have any particularly attractive taste or body. It is watery sweetened rice powder. It doesn't have foam or froth well.

Soya - Soya milk is very versatile and available sweetened, unsweetened, and with added flavors like vanilla and chocolate. It froths really well and has a lovely silky smooth texture. Some brands of soya milk can impart a strong bean taste, so shop around and find your preferred brand, or make it at home. Heating past 55°C (131°F) can deteriorate the taste, best to experiment with your ideal temperature. Soya is great with all coffee drinks, hot and cold, but don't drink too much (especially if you're a guy) as it messes with your hormones.

WATER

Good communication is just as stimulating as black coffee, and just as hard to sleep after.
- Anne Morrow Lindbergh (Author)

One of the most important elements to your coffee is probably not what you thought. As coffee consists of up to 98% water, it's no wonder that this ingredient plays a vital role. In this chapter, we look at how water, milk, and sugar affect the taste of your coffee.

Water
As water quality varies by region, it's essential to take this into account. For example, if the composition of minerals contained in the water is not balanced, the aroma cannot fully develop. Water quality is of central importance to the machine you're using as well. Using a water filter prevents the scale deposits building up on your machine which can lead to breakdowns.

Water Hardness
Ideal coffee water is fresh and pure in taste and has no discernible odors. It should be mineral- rich, so distilled water is not ideal. It must have a balanced mineral content. Only then can coffee develop that full aroma.

'Hard water' has high levels of mineral hardness (calcium and magnesium ions). That is what causes scale build up around your taps, in your kettle, and in coffee machines. You have to treat the hardness to get the best flavor and to keep your equipment in good order.

If you live in a hard water area (find out online), then you need to use a filter to 'soften' your water.

Chlorine
Water utility companies everywhere are required to provide water that is safe to drink. They need to ensure that water is free from pathogens that could make people sick. Chlorine is used to keep water 'safe and clean,' the same way it is used in swimming pools. Chlorine is a noticeable odor in a lot of tap water, and nobody wants that in their coffee.

If your tap water contains unwanted odors or a strong chemical taste, you probably already drink bottled water. In that case, only use bottled water for your coffee brewing as well.

Balanced PH
The pH value, from the Latin potentia hydrogenii, i.e. "the power of hydrogen," describes the concentration of hydrogen ions in a liquid. This determines whether water is acid, neutral or alkaline in chemical terms.

The pH value of a substance is measured on a scale of 0 to 14. Pure water has a neutral value of 7.0. Lower values indicate that a liquid is acid, higher values that it is alkaline. Colas have a pH value of 2.3, for tomato juice it is 4.0 and for lemon juice 2.5.

The pH value of the drinking water provided by our water authorities is between 5.5 and 9.5, depending on the country. PH plays a big part in the way we experience coffee. Water with neutral PH of 7 means that you will extract a balanced taste from your coffee beans.

Acid or alkaline water will throw the flavors out.

Water Filter Cartridges
Using filtered water has the benefit of protecting the equipment you use, and reduces the amount of maintenance required. When you are investing in a quality coffee machine, you need to make sure you look after it as much as possible. Filtered water will also improve the aroma and body of the coffee you make, regardless of using a steeping, dripping or pressure method.

There are many water filtration systems for the home out there. Brita is a well-known brand available worldwide that uses carbon cartridges to filter tap water. A Brita water filter is an easy and efficient way of reducing the carbonate hardness, chlorine (if present) and lead/copper. Personally, I don't like the way water tastes when using the Brita filter, but there are similar alternatives available that do pretty much the same thing. What I love about these water systems is that they
are inexpensive and easy to use, especially if you do not want to or cannot fit an integrated water filtration system into your home.

Cartridges are straightforward and easy to manage, you only need to replace them every few months. I had to try a few different brands to find the one that produced the water to suit my taste, but I found that any of the filters I tried produced a better cup of coffee than just using regular tap water.

More Information
Your local water company should be able to give you detailed information about the composition of your tap water. Check online, as most water utility companies have a website where you can access the information directly. Alternatively, call or write to your supplier.

In the US: http://water.epa.gov/drink/local/ In the UK: http://www.water.org.uk/

SUGAR AND SWEETENERS

Sugar also plays a major role in coffee consumption. Most people prefer to take sugar in their coffee, whether drinking filter or Espresso. Some coffee purists may scoff at the idea of tainting their coffee with sugar, but it is all about what you like. We can say that an excellent coffee can be sipped without any sugar, a moderate quality coffee could do with some sweetening, and a bad coffee must have milk and sugar both.

Most people probably add sugar to counter the bitterness of the coffee. Bitterness is kind of innate to coffee, so we cannot get rid of it. Even after adding sugar, you will still taste the bitterness. Some have a palate for bitterness and can appreciate it along with the other aromas in the cup.

So which sugar do you prefer? White or brown? Demerara? Or sweetener? Refined white sugar adds sweetness without any other taste. Dark brown sugar adds a syrupy and caramel-like taste alongside the added sweetness.

What about sweetening with honey? Or sweetened condensed milk? Or caramel syrup? Try different things and use what works best for you.

PART SEVEN
BREW THE PERFECT COFFEE

COFFEE BREWING

Coffee is a language in itself. - Jackie Chan (actor and martial artist)

While most of us enjoy a fresh cup of coffee in the morning, many of us do not understand the mechanics at work for the creation of an excellent cup of joe. Brewing coffee may be a complex process, but it doesn't necessarily have to be.

The following methods all aim to do the same thing; to extract the desirable coffee solubles from the ground and roasted beans, leave the unwanted bits (both soluble and insoluble) behind, producing an enjoyable cup of coffee. Did you know that 18-22% of extraction is considered desirable?

By the end of this chapter you should be able to understand:
- The different types of equipment and general methods that are needed to brew coffee.
- The differences between the 'drip,' 'steep' and 'high pressure' brewing methods.
- Understand about the percentage of bean that goes into the actual cup and what kind of flavors is considered desirable or undesirable.
- Become familiar with the terms – 'under-' and 'over extraction.'

DRIP BREWED COFFEE

One of the most common and straightforward methods for brewing is by dripping or pouring water on coffee grounds sitting on a filter. The water extracts the good stuff from the coffee grounds and passes through the filter leaving the spent coffee grounds behind, making a lovely clean cup of coffee. Filter coffee is characterized for being less bitter and more rounded than an Espresso. Also brighter and more full-bodied than an Americano. An Americano is an Espresso based drink.

Filtered coffee is the end product of water passing slowly through the medium-coarse ground coffee to drip into the container below. Freshly brewed filter coffee offers body that other methods cannot match. The drip method is responsible for its depth of flavor.

An individual cup of filtered coffee made using the pour-over method requires quality coffee grounds, a filter, and a cup. You will also need a filter cone to hold the filter. These can be bought online, and are usually made of either plastic or porcelain.

There are several different kinds of filters available for use with a filter cone or a drip machine: paper, cloth, screen, and metal filter and each has their own characteristics (more details in chapter 4).

General Tips

Consider the following when preparing filter coffee:

Grind: Medium - like sand or granulated sugar. Too fine and you will find paper filters get clogged, too coarse and you will end up with weak under-extracted coffee.

Water to Coffee Ratio: Weigh out 6-10 grams per cup of coffee, or use about one rounded teaspoon per cup. Making a pot, use about 100 grams per liter of water.

Brew Time: A single cup filter should take approximately 3 minutes. Patience required as you slowly pour the water over the filter! Using a machine, it should take about 6 minutes to make a liter.

Water Temperature: The water temperature should range between 92-96°C (197-206°F), never boiling! If you are heating water in a kettle or pot, bring it to the boil, then turn off the heat, and allow it to rest a little before pouring over your coffee grounds.

Brew Turbulence: Give it a little turbulence to help extraction. Start to pour in enough water to about halfway. Then stir for a few seconds to aid extraction. Continue to pour the water over slowly.

Examples of Filter Coffee Equipment:

Filter coffee machine

Automatic filter coffee machines may be to blame for the bad reputation that persists in some countries. Widely used in hotels and convenience stores, filter coffee can sit for hours in the carafe growing stale and burning off all the lovely aromatics. As with all coffee, freshness is important.

If you leave filter coffee on the heating element, it will lose its freshness after 10-15 minutes, after which it acquires a bitter burnt taste. It is best practice to pour it into a vacuum flask so that it will retain it's fresh taste for up to an hour.

Using a filter machine is simple, just add the amount of water into the tank. Always use fresh filtered water. Insert a clean and wet filter into the cone - some machines contain a reusable filter, so just ensure it is clean. Add enough coffee and let it do the rest! Filter coffee machines are available with a built-in grinder and are referred to as 'bean to cup' filter machines.

V60, Clever, Woodneck

These three devices work in the same way yet they each have their set of characteristics. The V60 and Clever use paper filters and the Woodneck uses cloth. This brewing method is excellent for single origin lighter roasts, producing an aromatic, clean cup of coffee without any sediment.

The V60 and Clever are affordably priced pieces of kit. Both of these are extremely simple to use. Simply place the brewer over a cup or mug, and pour water from a kettle into the coffee ground. A cool thing about the Clever is that it contains a little mechanism that holds the water in the cone, allowing you to add additional extraction time. You then release the mechanism and allow the coffee to drip into your mug.

The mid-priced Woodneck device uses a cloth sock-like filter which produces a clear tasting brew. The cloth allows oils that would be trapped in a paper filter to pass through, yet retains all the sediment. Maintaining the filter can be a hassle. You need to keep it wet at all times, either storing it in a cup of water or a plastic bag.

All three of these devices work in the same way. Start with fresh filtered water that you boil in your kettle or pan. Always wet your filter and place in the cone. Run some of your boiled water into your cup or through the

Woodneck, which will help keep the coffee hot while waiting for all of it to drip through.

Measure or weigh your coffee and add to the filter. Add enough water to cover the grounds and give it time to 'bloom,' 20 to 30 seconds should suffice. If using the Clever, you have an advantage here, as you can control how long the water will stay in the cone!

Adding a bit more water and giving it a stir to help achieve an even extraction. Continue pouring slowly using a circular and even motion. It will take about a minute and a half to complete. Once the dripping stops you are done! You can rinse or discard your filter and enjoy your cup of coffee.

Using these devices allows you to experiment making small changes to the water to coffee ratios, grind size, brew temperature, turbulence and time to achieve your ideal cup.

STEEP BREWED COFFEE

Steeping or macerating means soaking in water. Using this method will allow the water to extract as much as possible from the coffee grounds. Tea is also prepared by steeping, and the same principles apply. The hot water will release the flavor and nutrients, and a filter will hold the grounds back. Steeping ground coffee is also very simple, and again you don't need much equipment. In fact, you can prepare coffee right at the table in front of your guests.

Steeped coffee has unique flavor characteristics and is the preferred method for millions of people. It tastes similar to drip coffee except it contains added richness which comes from using metal filters. And because the coffee grounds remain in contact with the hot water for longer, additional flavors which are harder to extract can be found. You can expect a bolder body, and since metallic mesh filters are commonly used, you can also expect plenty of residue at the bottom of your cup.

The main issue faced by this method is that you must keep control of the brew time more carefully than with filter coffee. If you leave it too long, you will have bitter coffee. Not enough time and you'll have weak coffee.

General Tips

Consider the following when preparing steeped coffee:

Grind: Coarse - chunky like rock salt. A good grinder using fresh beans will minimize the fine powdery stuff typical of older beans. Going too fine and you will find end up with over extracted bitterness with masses of sludge in your cup.

Water to Coffee Ratio: Weigh out 6 grams per cup, or use about one rounded teaspoon per cup, similar to filter coffee. Calculate about 100 grams per liter of water.

Brew Time: Steep the coffee grounds for about 3-4 minutes.

Water Temperature: The water temperature should range between 92-96°C (197-206°F), never boiling! If you are heating water in a kettle or pot, bring it to the boil, then turn off the heat, and allow it to rest a little before pouring over your coffee grounds.

Brew Turbulence: It will require a good stir of about 10 seconds to ensure even extraction.

Cafetière

The Cafetière, also called French Press, Plunger or Press Pot, is a really simple piece of kit that is widely available. A Cafetière usually comes with a little measuring scoop and a built-in metal filter. Clean up, and maintenance are easy too. As with filter coffee, if you are not going to drink the whole pot within 10 minutes of prep, pour the coffee into a thermal jug to keep it fresh.

To get a perfect result using a Cafetière, start with fresh filtered water that you boil in your kettle or pan. Add some water into the Cafetière to warm it up, leave the plunger to the side for now. Dose your coffee and place it into the Cafetière. You can either weigh it up or use the scoop provided; it's recommended to do one scoop per cup (so if you have an 8 cup Cafetière, and you are making a full pot you should start with eight scoops). You may like it a little weaker or stronger, so as always find the dosage that suits your taste.

Add your water to the vessel and be sure to get everything nicely mixed up. Allow it to infuse for 3-4 minutes. Now give it a good stir for about 10 seconds before using the plunger. Be careful; you don't want to cause a spill or burn yourself! Plunge slowly and deliberately, pushing the filter down to the bottom of the vessel to contain all the coffee grounds away from the coffee. Allow a few seconds before you serve or pour into a holding flask or jug.

Eva Solo

The Eva Solo is a lovely piece of kit! The same concept as a Cafetière, the coarse ground coffee is steeped in hot water for a short amount of time. So what's different? The Eva Solo is a beautiful piece of kit, it's got a clever pouring spout, and you do not need to plunge, so you save 1 step on the Cafetière. It also has a heat retaining cover which keeps your coffee warm for longer! You should still pour it into a flask or jug if you plan on drinking over a longer period.

Cold Brewed Coffee

Cold brewing is a steeping method which doesn't use heat, hence the name. Using very coarse ground coffee, you simply allow it to steep in water for 12 hours or longer. You use cold or room temperature water. The grounds must be filtered after steeping the same as other steeping methods.

Cold brew produces a strong coffee elixir that must be diluted before serving. There lies the magic
- dilute it with cold ingredients for a proper cold coffee. Dilute with hot ingredients for a different take on your usual hot coffee. You can dilute with whatever you fancy; it is so versatile!

Cold brewed coffee has a lower acidity and bitterness than coffee made using hot water; you get a much smoother coffee. Iced coffees should only be made with cold brewed concentrate, taking an Espresso and pouring it over ice is just wrong! Keep in mind that the same coffee beans prepared using a cold brew method will not have the same notes and taste as if you used a hot method. You may be surprised! Another advantage with cold brew is that you can store it in your fridge for up to a week without harming the taste so that it could be a real time saver.

General Tips

Consider the following when preparing cold brewed coffee:

Grind: Very coarse - chunky like rock salt.

Water to Coffee Ratio: Calculate about 100 grams per 400ml of water. Remember you are making a coffee concentrate.

Brew Time: From 10-14 hours. Overnight works well!

Water Temperature: Room temperature.

Brew Turbulence: Stir to ensure all the grounds are wet.

Cold brewing is really easy; you don't need much regarding equipment. You can even repurpose your Cafetière for cold brewing. After the coffee has steeped, you can filter your coffee through screen and into another vessel. You will want to filter it a bit more, using either a cloth filter, paper filter or a fine-mesh filter.

Keep your coffee concentrate in the fridge and dilute with hot water for a different take on Americano. However, cold brew really shines for iced drinks. Start with a ratio of 1 part concentrate to 2 parts water or milk and check how that suits your taste.

HIGH-PRESSURE EXTRACTION/ESPRESSO

Espresso, a full bodied and rich instant coffee! The idea for inventing an Espresso came from the need for instant coffee. The idea is to speed up the process of hot water passing through the coffee ground. The most obvious way to do this is using pressure. This is the result of the industrial revolution and the steam engine being applied to the humble coffee bean.

Using extra fine ground coffee and either a pump or steam Espresso machine you obtain a rich syrupy, intensely flavored coffee. Steam under pressure is used to maximize extraction. Characterized by bold flavor and a foam (the results of the pressure) called coffee crema. It's used as a base for long drinks; it's mixed with steamed milk to increase the richness of the beverage.

The next chapter is all about the Espresso machine. It is important to know that there are other ways to get Espresso, read on!

General Tips

Consider the following when preparing Espresso coffee (the following is the standard for an Italian Espresso):

Grind: Fine - smooth to the touch. Adjusting the grind size will alter the time in the basket - refer to the Grind section for more info.

Water to Coffee Ratio: Weigh out 7-10 grams per Espresso. Good grinders have additional features that help maintain dosage consistency.

Brew Time: 25 seconds to produce a 25ml shot.

Water Temperature: The water temperature is 90°C (194°F) at 9 bars of pressure.

Brew Turbulence: The coffee grounds are packed tightly in a small basket, but it's the pressure that ensures an even extraction.

Examples of Espresso Coffee Equipment

Aeropress

None of the hand powered methods are as instant as Steam Espresso machine. The Aeropress Coffee and Espresso maker makes rich, smooth and flavorsome coffee in only one minute and it takes just seconds to clean up afterward. The Aeropress is like the more familiar cafetière, you put in the coffee, add water, and stir but you don't need to wait for the coffee to brew before pressing down the plunger. The plunger seal is designed to make air pressure in the chamber build up, which shortens the filtering time and squeezes additional flavor from the coffee. It is an affordable way to make Espresso. The device sits directly on a mug or cup, like a drip brewer, and consists of a plastic chamber with a screw-on filter on the bottom and a plunger with a seal. It uses it's own micro-filters that allow the right amount of oils to pass through to achieve the taste of an Espresso. You cannot obtain the crema a good Espresso machine can produce, due to the lower amount of pressure. True Espresso aficionados may miss the crema, but you can still create latte and Cappuccinos using the Espresso from the Aerobie.

Grind: Fine - smooth to the touch for Espresso. Use medium to achieve an excellent filter coffee.

Water to Coffee Ratio: You can weigh up or use the scoop provided, one scoop per cup.

Brew Time: Less than a minute.

Water Temperature: Use freshly boiled water, just let it rest a bit after it reaches the boiling point.

Brew Turbulence: Use the stirrer provided and stir for about 10 seconds before plunging.

Handpresso

The Handpresso is a mobile Espresso maker that requires a good amount of effort to make excellent Espresso. At a quick glance you might think it is something you would find in a head shop in Amsterdam, but rest assured this is a coffee making device. With the Handpresso, you create the pressure rather than relying on steam-powered pressure systems of traditional Espresso makers.

You pump the device around 40 times to create 16 bars of pressure, then add hot water into the holding bulb. You use a coffee pod in the compartment and simply press the button to release the pressure and serve your Espresso. This is a travel Espresso device and using pods means that clean up is virtually none.

ROK Espresso

The ROK is attractive; it is a great piece of design that would look awesome on your kitchen counter and would really impress guests at a dinner party. It makes real Espresso but not without some fuss and tinkering. It works just like the Aeropress, just with more power!

The ROK comes with a portafilter just like you would find on a traditional Espresso machine. You dose your coffee and tamp it using the scoop (which doubles as a tamper) then position it into the device. This will take a bit of getting used to before you can do it all quickly.

You add your hot water at the top, then you press the arms downwards to create pressure and brew your Espresso. You will need the practice to end up with well-extracted coffee since pushing the arms too quickly can easily result in under-extracted coffee. The manufacturer suggests that you can get between 5-10 bar of pressure depending on how hard you squeeze the handles down.

The ROK creates a pleasant, slightly above average Espresso, which will wow people as you make Espresso at the dinner table. It takes practice to achieve consistent results, and it is not as simple as other methods.

Nespresso/A Modo Mio

Instant fully automatic Espresso 'pod' machines have gained a lot of popularity recently. These machines have an excellent reputation for the consistency of the Espressos they produce. Nespresso pretty much created this new market and still dominates. The adverts featuring George Clooney are pretty classic.

Using the pod system couldn't be easier. You turn on the machine, add fresh water to the tank, insert your pod, and get your Espresso fix in about 30 seconds. It is a clever system which uses these pods to keep the coffee fresh until use. All the settings are pre-set on the machine, you simply plug it in and away you go.

The downside of a capsule-only machine, such as Nespresso or A Modo Mio, is the cost per shot of coffee. This works out nearly four times more expensive per shot than using ground coffee or coffee beans.

Find out about each of these brewing methods by visiting www.boldbarista.com

PART EIGHT
SUSTAINABILITY

PROTECTING WHAT WE LOVE

Today it is possible to find good coffee in every major city in the world, from London to Sydney to Tokyo; we are drinking more and, more importantly, better coffee. The importance of coffee to the global economy cannot be overstated. It is one of the most valuable primary products in world trade, in many years second in value only to oil as a source of foreign exchange to producing countries. - International Coffee Organisation

Coffee farmers the world over are at the bottom of the coffee supply chain. When we, the consumers, purchase coffee at retail barely less than %10 of the sale price will be going to the farmers. Most of the money generated from coffee goes to traders, marketers, roasters and governments collecting a tax. Its cultivation, processing, trading, transportation and marketing provide employment for hundreds of millions of people worldwide.

There are about 25 million coffee producers in the world, many of them only having a few acres of land. Individual farmers sell their crop to local agents or cooperatives - just four big traders control
%40 of the world's coffee, selling onwards international companies. Billions of consumers then purchase the end product at retail.

The price of coffee is set at the commodity exchanges in London and New York; prices can vary from a low of 34 US cents per pound in 2001 to 309 cents in 2011. As with any other commodity, the price fluctuations are caused by many factors such as speculation (futures), over production, demand, adverse weather. Such high variations in price mean it's hard for farmers to know what kind of income to expect.

Demand for coffee worldwide is indeed increasing, and it is important for us consumers to be aware of the effects of our buying habits. Many coffee farms are in areas regarded as high priorities for conservation, in fact, much of the land used for coffeeagriculture was carved out of what was once a rainforest. Many times this property was taken violently from the indigenous people who have no way to protect themselves.

COFFEE RUST

We mentioned that Robusta coffee plants are hardier to climate, they can grow perfectly in direct sunlight for example. The Robusta plant is also resistant to the fungus which causes leaf rust. This helps to paint a bigger picture of coffee cultivation throughout the world. Those farmers whose Arabica crops were blighted by the fungus may have felt relief when they discovered that they could cultivate Robusta coffee plants instead.

In the final decades of the 19th century, this affliction practically wiped out the coffee plantations across South East Asia, particularly Sri Lanka, Philippines, and Java. More recently since 2012, numerous Central American countries have been fighting to keep coffee rust under control.

Countries like Guatemala, Honduras, Mexico and Peru all have national programs in place to invest in research and develop better systems to eradicate the fungus.

Is there anything else we can do to protect Arabica plantations? Does the answer lie in training and education for coffee farmers, and in changing the way farms are managed? Or do we just need to develop the right kind of fungicide, whether synthetic or organic to combat this fungus?

ORGANIC AND OTHER CERTIFICATIONS

Many of us understand sustainable agriculture as the prohibition of synthetic agrochemicals, but many of the certification schemes allow certain synthetics to be used. Even 'organic' labeled products allow some synthetic agro-chemical use.

We have to look further than just the agricultural aspect, most of the certification organizations also include standards for nature conservation through the prohibition of clearing primary ecosystems. Some focus on protecting biodiversity and soil and water conservation, while others place a stronger focus on the prohibition of the use of genetically modified organisms. Others on diversity in crop production and maintenance of soil fertility and biological activity.

Although there are many criticisms placed on each of the schemes, it's hard for us to assess the real impact, if any, they will help to achieve in the longer term. What real evidence do we have that demonstrates any difference this type of model is making in those local communities, except what the organizations themselves offer?

These labels on your coffee will usually mean you have to pay a premium but are they just marketing tools to take your money? Are they simply ways to make you 'feel better' about your purchase? Do any of these certification schemes place the coffee bean and the farmer at the heart of the matter?

UTZ CERTIFIED

UTZ was founded in 2002 as a labeling program for sustainably farmed agricultural products, at the moment it focuses on coffee, cocoa, tea, and palm oil. Buying UTZ Certified coffee, cocoa or tea means that you are 'helping to build a better future,' or so they say. The UTZ program enables training for farmers to learn how to improve their farming methods, their working conditions. They emphasize the importance of education for children and the need to care for the environment.

Their code of conduct is a set of criteria that 'certified' farms must adhere to: such as efficient farm management and sustainable and responsible methods of farming including standards for record keeping, minimized and documented use of agrochemicals for crop protection, protection of labour rights and access to health care and education for employees and their families. They state their aim is to enable sustainable farming as the norm. Coffee producers who are 'certified' are subject to annual inspections by independent certifiers to ensure they comply with the criteria.

UTZ do not charge any fees to coffee producers, and UTZ does not guarantee a minimum price like other certification schemes do. However, UTZ certified produce does demand a higher price at
market. The main criticism on UTZ certification is the fact that they do not ban the use of artificial fertilizers or pesticides.

Possibly the unique aspect of UTZ is the fact that all aspects of the supply chain are traceable to the end customer via a system that is accessible on their website. You can use it to follow the coffee along the chain from grower to cup, giving us consumers an insight into the journey our coffee takes to reach us. The fees generated by the use of this traceability system make a large sum of UTZ's income. Additionally, they receive funds and subsidies from several government organizations and NGOs.

FAIRTRADE

Fairtrade is an international system which aims to empower farmers and to inform consumers. They work with farmer cooperatives and guarantee their members a stable price for their crops, so if the international price falls, at least the members will be able to rely on a minimum sale price for their crop. If the global price is higher than the minimum, they will pay the higher price plus a premium. Fairtrade aims for farmers to be paid enough to cover their costs plus to invest in their farms, and to 'secure a stable future for their families.'

Fairtrade establishes standards for producers to create sustainable farming methods to protect the natural ecosystems from degrading and that land is used sustainably. There are also labor practice standards, for example, they prohibit child labor in their cooperatives.

As a consumer, seeing the Fairtrade Mark means you have an assurance that farmers are getting a 'fair' deal for their work. But what does 'fair' mean to you? There is a lot of criticism for Fairtrade and their model because of the interpretation of this word.

While many in the West believe in eliminating poverty, critics say that Fairtrade only aims to keep farmers poor over the long term. Why? Well someone has to grow and pick those beans cheaply so we can continue to drink our lattes, right? How much of the additional money charged to the consumer reaches the farmer? What evidence do we have any impact on the local farmer's communities?

ORGANIC

Everything 'organic' has become very popular in the last ten years. Widely believed to be healthier, tastier and just better, the term 'organic' is directly used to address the growing demand from consumers for produce free from synthetic chemical and genetically modified organisms.

Produce labeled as organic can only come from farms that have been certified organic and meet certain requirements that may involve production standards for growing, processing and shipping. There is no internationally recognized 'Organic Certification,' and these requirements vary from country to country. Some countries do not have government regulation for the use of the term and rely on private businesses.

The requirements for the UK Soil Association certification include avoiding the use of certain fertilizers and pesticides as detailed on a list of prohibited chemicals, the farmland to be certified must also be free from these chemicals for at least three years before the first 'organic' harvest.

Certification also means the farms will be having on-site inspections periodically.

There are many criticisms for organic as a label. Some claim it leads to a misunderstanding in consumers' minds, leading us to think that organic means 'higher quality'. Most people believe 'organic' means that agrochemicals aren't being used, but in fact, there is a list of allowed chemicals. There is a growing concern that labeling is replacing education and information. People who think they are making educated choices end up placing too much trust in the label.

RAINFOREST ALLIANCE

The Rainforest Alliance is an American charity founded in 1987 with the aim of conserving biodiversity and informing the public about the destruction of the world's forests. Currently, their work reaches over 70 countries. It helped to found the Forest Stewardship Council, which is recognized as the world's most rigorous forestry operations standards.

To become a certified farm, you must meet criteria regarding reducing agrochemical usage, protecting waterways, conserving biodiversity and ecosystems and protection of local workers.

Some of the key differentiators from other certification schemes are the concern over the workers at the farms. Farmers must provide protective gear for their workers and child labor is not allowed.

Farmers must pay a decent wage to their workers and treat them with respect. They claim that all employees at certified farms can count on decent housing, safe drinking water, school for their children, and healthcare services. The organization aims to assist with training improving the way the land is used to sustain the ecosystems that exist in the local areas, and by conserving preventing the degradation of the environment.

The Rainforest Alliance certification has also come under criticism, the most damning of which calls it "Fairtrade light" because it is cheaper than the most popular alternative. Critics say it offers big companies like Kraft and McDonald's a cheap way to reach ethical consumers, answering their concerns for sustainably sourced goods. Rainforest Alliance does not offer a minimum price to coffee producers, but it does pay above the market price. Minimum price programs are much criticized by economists, and Rainforest Alliance aims to add value by helping the coffee producers improve their yields and use their land more efficiently. The organization allows companies to use the seal in their packaging and marketing when only as little as 30% of the product is being sourced from certified producers. This adds to the criticism that this organization is only helping large enterprises market themselves to a particular demographic, and not really about helping reduce the problems in the developing world.

DIRECT TRADE & SINGLE ORIGIN

In addition to the certification schemes mentioned above, nowadays it is becoming more common to find that coffee is being traded directly with the farmer and using its origin as a marketing angle. Direct trade means that the coffee is being sourced directly from the grower. Companies who choose to do this, promise to ensure that farmers are paid fairly. On the positive side, this practice can allow coffee businesses to work with the producers to establish more sustainable practices. On the downside, the consumer is reliant on these organizations to audit their work in dealing with the coffee growers.

Single origin means that coffee comes from one particular region or even a single producer. Again, there is no body of governance to oversee the use of this term, and it is often up to interpretation. Some companies use it to refer to coffee from a single plantation; others use it about a blend from an individual region. But of course, it may also mean that it is coffee from a single country.

The single origin label does certainly give the coffee a more upmarket appearance which is usually reflected in the higher price. Be aware that it may not necessarily mean higher quality or better taste. Later on in this book, we look at how we taste coffee and how tasting coffee from single origins helps us learn to identify the beans flavors.

FIND OUT MORE

Thank you for reading!

Visit our blog at www.boldbarista.com to find a collection of 22 tried and tested recipes to try at home, stay up to date, and learn more about coffee.

Printed in Great Britain
by Amazon